Ding Bat And His Happy Flying Friends

John and Evalen Cruzan

Illustrated by Avery Liell-Kok

AuthorHouse™
1663 Liberty Drive
Bloomington, IN 47403
www.authorhouse.com
Phone: 1-800-839-8640

First published by AuthorHouse   9/29/2011

ISBN: 978-1-4670-3982-6 (sc)

Library of Congress Control Number: 2011917314

Printed in the United States of America

Any people depicted in stock imagery provided by Thinkstock are models,
and such images are being used for illustrative purposes only.
Certain stock imagery © Thinkstock.

This book is printed on acid-free paper.

Because of the dynamic nature of the Internet, any web addresses or links contained in this book may have changed
since publication and may no longer be valid. The views expressed in this work are solely those of the author and do
not necessarily reflect the views of the publisher, and the publisher hereby disclaims any responsibility for them.

authorHOUSE®

Dedication

This book is dedicated to the memory of John's deceased wife Monica (who tolerated the stories) and to his children, Donna, Debra and David, to whom he told bat stories when they were young when they asked for a good night story. It is also dedicated to his older grandchildren, Tejay, Kaycee and Jaycey and to the littlest ones, Joshua, Jonathan and Joseph, in hopes they like the latest story.

John and Evalen Cruzan

*O*nce upon a time there was a special bat family, Mama Bat, Papa Bat and Ding Bat. They lived with a zillion other bats under the Congress Avenue Bridge in Austin, Texas.

My name is Grandpa Bat and I live with Grandma Bat and I am telling of the adventures of our grandson Ding Bat. He will be dropping by with some of his friends for some snacks and a little story time.

Beep beep, burp burp, chirp chirp!!! "Oh Grandma, I can hear him -- Ding's here now!"

"Home of Grandpa and Grandma Bat"

"Hey Grandpa, meet my friends, Memyah Bat, Peachy Bat and Acro Bat. Memyah Bat is my special gurl friend. Grandpa, I'm crazy about her and I want to marry her someday. She makes me feel so funny and silly. Peachy Bat is my new friend. He got separated from his family under the bridge so we asked him to fly with us. He is a fruit bat. We are teaching him to catch insects and he is going to teach us to eat fruit. Acro Bat has been teaching us some fancy flying so we can catch those tricky moths. Wow Grandpa, he can turn on a dime and do somersaults and gets them every time! Now Grandpa, tell us a story, tell us where we came from."

"Meet My Friends"

"Well Ding, that is a verry good story. I think you will enjoy it. God created us on the 5th day and we are flying mammals. That means we have babies called pups and nurse them with bat milk. He also created insects for us to eat – pretty good so far???"

"Well Grandpa, I was thinking more like how did we get to Austin, Texas, to live under the bridge?"

"Oh! Now that's another good story. Weeell, we were living in and flying in and out of a cave not too far away but there were too many of us to live in the cave. There were bazillions of us and the cave was getting crowded.

"Now this happened in 1980, I was young and not married to your Grandma yet. The Bat Council, full of wise old bats, decided we needed a new place to live so they went searching for a new roost.

"Wow!! They spotted this Congress Avenue Bridge that was just finished. The old bats looked it over and told everyone, "Tomorrow, come in early from insect chasing and be ready for a long journey before dawn. We are moving, so pack up your things and gather your pups."

"Home at Congress Avenue Bridge"

"So Ding, a big black cloud of zillions of bats took over the bridge and called it home. It was on the lake so there were lots of bugs to eat and everyone had a place to roost for the summer. You remember making the flight, don't you Ding?"

"Yes, Grandpa. Wow, that was quite a long flying lesson! I was so little then and sort of scared so I was glad Mama and Papa Bat were flying close by. I was so tired my wings would hardly move."

Grandma Bat came in bringing a plate of insects and fruit nectar. She gave them hugs and kisses and said, "Now you sweet little bats, you eat every bit of these snacks so you will sleep all day and be ready to work all night."

"Okay Grandma, we will and Grandpa, we will be back tomorrow for the rest of the story. We are off to our roost."

Beep beep, burp burp, chirp chirp, "Hi Grandpa Bat, we're back!"

"Wow Grandpa, we had quite a nite! We swooped out of the roost in one black cloud and below us was a boat full of humans gawking at us and yelling in a strange language."

"That's English," Grandpa said, "that's how they talk. You may have heard some Spanish too. That's mostly what you hear in Mexico where we will be flying back to in November. But we all talk in chirps and squeaks and all of our family understands."

"Well Grandpa, we made 2 more passes over a big boat and there was lots of excitement. We wanted to get those pesky squitos that were over the lake so Acro Bat showed us a new trick of flying through a big bunch of squitos. We'd open our wings and catch a big bunch of them under our wings. Then we would fly with our heads under our wings and eat them. It was really funny – we would weave all over the place cuz we weren't watching how we were flying -- it was lots of fun. Then we flew over the boat again and found a produce stand. Peachy was hungry so we had to find him some fruit. Grandpa, why is that big boat on the lake?"

"Dinner on the Lake"

"Good question Ding. You remember your Papa's friend, Inventor Bat? Well, he was very smart and invented a special battery that could run the boat. Since humans are very clever at making money and we are the largest colony of Urban Bats around, they told everyone about us. Then people paid to ride in the boat to watch us while we flew out from under the bridge. The people of Austin were very happy as they made lots of money from the boat rides and also they had free insect removal."

"Ding, people thought we were so special that they flew into the city on planes just to come and watch us fly. Also, many big humans and little humans would bring blankets and sit on the hill by the bridge, waiting just to see us fly from our roosts.

"Well Little Bats, Grandma has some treats for us. Grandmas are like that – they like to spoil us. Now off to your roosts. Ding, you watch out for Memyah Bat. If she can't find her Mama and Papa Bat, you'll need to watch over her and protect her. And, Ding, be sure you watch out for owls, our enemies. They have been trying to eat us for a long time."

"Oh I will Grandpa. We'll play awhile then I'll make sure she finds a safe roost for the day. I'll ask Mama and Papa Bat if we can come back tomorrow to see you and Grandma."

When Ding and his friends returned, Ding was shouting, "Grandpa, Grandma, Mama just told us that she is going to have a baby in a couple of weeks. We were all excited and we promised her that we would help raise the pup. We told her we would find her the pesky corn moths that make good bat milk that has lots of vitamins."

"Baby Pup is to be Born"

Grandpa said, "Gather around and I'll tell you where to find them. They fly high like the airplanes you see, so just go up high and you will find them and then bring them back to your Mama to eat. These moths eat a lot of the human's good food so the humans will like it if we can get a lot of the moths for her to eat. It protects their crops.

"Your Mama will have her pup in June and will carry it around for 5 days. Then she will leave it at the roost while she hunts for food. But you guys are going to help her -- right?"

"Yeah," they all said, "we are going to help!!"

"Now the baby will be born hairless and pink and will grow very fast. Remember it will be flying with you in 5 weeks so teach it well. Then all of you and the pup need to eat extra food for our long flight when we all go back to Mexico."

"Flight to Find Special Corn Moths"

"Okay Grandpa, we will remember that."

Grandpa said, "Okay, here comes Grandma. Let's see if she has any yummy snacks for us tonight."

"I'm sorry," Grandma said, "I'm out of Bat Cakes today. I'll try to get some more made so I'll have them for you next time."

"Okay Grandma, we're going back to the bridge now. So save some Bat Cakes for us because they are yum yum good!"

Soon a "beep beep, burp burp, chirp chirp" was heard and off flew Ding Bat and his happy flying friends.

About the Authors

John Cruzan and Evalen Petrich graduated in 1957 from Bethel High School at Spanaway, Washington. John was Editor of Brave Talk, the school paper, and Evalen was the Associate Editor. Fifty-three years later they were in contact again and John told Evalen that he had always considered writing a children's book. He told her that he used to tell his children, when they wanted a good night story, a story that always started with "Once upon a time there were 3 bats, Mama Bat, Papa Bat and Ding Bat." Then he took it in any direction in order to amuse them. Evalen said "Well, why don't you do it now?" Well, John woke up very early the next day and started excitedly writing down ideas. He called Evalen and told her what he had been doing. She said "Great, did you know that here in Austin, Texas, there are 1.5 million bats that live under the Congress Avenue Bridge in downtown Austin?" John didn't know that and thought Austin would be a great place for Ding Bat to live. They started working on the story together over the phone. John took a trip to Austin to see the bats. Long story short, they wrote this book together and got married in March 2011 and now both live in Austin.

John and Evalen Cruzan